T0012008

THE LITTLE BOOK OF

NIAGARA FALLS

Published in 2023 by OH!
An Imprint of Welbeck Non-Fiction Limited,
part of Welbeck Publishing Group.
Offices in: London – 20 Mortimer Street, London W1T 3JW
and Sydney – 205 Commonwealth Street, Surry Hills 2010
www.welbeckpublishing.com

Compilation text © Welbeck Non-Fiction Limited 2023
Design © Welbeck Non-Fiction Limited 2023

ISBN 978-1-80069-392-0

Compiled and written by: Malcolm Croft
Editorial: Victoria Denne
Project manager: Russell Porter
Design: Tony Seddon
Production: Jess Brisley

A CIP catalogue record for this book is available from the British Library

Printed in China

10 9 8 7 6 5 4 3 2 1

THE LITTLE BOOK OF
NIAGARA FALLS

NATURAL BEAUTY

CONTENTS

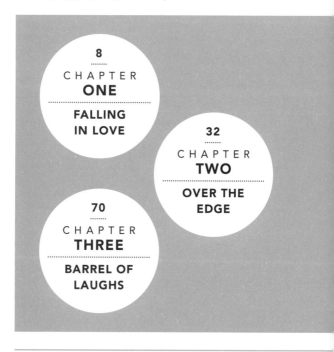

INTRODUCTION

Welcome to Niagara Falls! Drink in that view. It's a doozy. Who cares if you get soaked to the bone.

Now, Niagara's falls may not be the tallest, or the widest, or the deepest, or the loudest, or even the most remote waterfall in Mother Nature's dazzling array of global water features. But it is the most powerful. And fastest. And nothing is more attractive to the human eye than power and speed. It is the Muhammad Ali of water-based falling.

More volume of water flows over these thundering cliffs' edge faster than any other waterfall, mesmerising the millions of visitors a year who flock to see the fall and become locked into its lure, unable to look away. It is little wonder that the sheer all-encompassing beauty of this hotspot, and its surrounding State Park, is an icon that defines both home nations it proudly straddles, Canada and America, dazzling from sea to shining sea. Yes, this cataract attraction (see "Cataract", page 180) is a sight to behold in the mind's eye forever.

But, like all icons of nature, there is so much *more* to see, and do, and feel, and hear, at Niagara Falls than just get drenched in its awesome power. There's an immense history, both natural and man-made; there's ingenuity too, with technologies that lit up the world; and spirituality, in the legends and myths of its first residents; and, finally, there's bravery, in the hearts of the daredevils desperate to impress Mother Nature with their death-defying acts. There's also a gift shop at the exit for those looking for t-shirts, key rings, coffee mugs and other souvenirs to remember this unforgettable place. The world's love affair with nature tourism took flight here, after all.

The Little Book of Niagara Falls is a deep dive of all the waterfall-fun you can think of; a tiny tome packed with a thrilling feast of fast-flowing facts, stats, quotes, quips; a treasure trove of trivia and fun-sized brain snacks to keep you stuffed until tea-time.

So, pop on your poncho and prepare your barrel for laughs. It's time to go for a wild ride over the side…

CHAPTER
ONE

Falling in Love

Niagara Falls is the world's No.1 waterfall. It has everything. From rainbows to rapids, whirlpools to ponchos, and everything in between. All that's missing is you, so let's begin a fun amble across this great gorge and its amazing history where all good adventures start: the first step.

95

The volume, in decibels, of Niagara's thundering loudness.

That's as loud as a motorcycle engine running constantly. Any noise more than 85dB is considered VERY LOUD.

Niagara Falls is three waterfalls for the price of one.

Flowing north from Lake Erie, Niagara River is split by Goat Island – the majority of the river then flows towards the Horseshoe Falls, and the rest flows to the American Falls.

At the American Falls, the river is then divided again by Luna Island, which creates the third, small waterfall – Bridal Veil Falls.

2,509

The amount, in tons of force, of water that falls onto the rocks below the Horseshoe Falls.

That's 685,000 gallons of water per second (2,271,247 litres per second), or the equivalent weight of 40 average-sized houses falling on you.

At once.

66

The mere physical of Niagara
Falls is only this. Yet this is
really a very small part of that
world's wonder. It's power to
excite reflection, and emotion,
is its great charm.

99

Abraham Lincoln

66

I saw the Falls when I came here first in 1900. Do they look the same? Well, the principle seems the same. The water still keeps falling over.

99

Winston Churchill

66

There is an old saying that you have not seen any falls until you have seen Niagara Falls.

99

John F. Kennedy

Princess Elizabeth and her husband, Prince Philip, visited Niagara Falls in 1951, 20 months before Elizabeth would ascend to the throne to be crowned Her Majesty Queen Elizabeth II.

A crowd of 150,000
people cheered the
royal couple as they
soaked in the view. The
princess stood at the
railing of the Horseshoe
Falls and described the
view as "magnificent"
and "tremendous ".

If you fancy becoming one of the 50,00 daredevils who get married at Niagara Falls every year, simply call (716) 286-4392 to obtain your Marriage License (for a non-refundable fee of $150).

You'll meet lots of global
tourists at Niagara Falls,
so listen out for the word
"waterfall" in these languages:

1. *Cascada* – Catalan
2. *Slap* – Croatian
3. *Waterval* – Dutch
4. *Vesiputous* – Finnish
5. *Kosk* – Estonian
6. *Cascade* – French
7. *Wasserfall* – German
8. *Foss* – Icelandic
9. *Cascata* – Italian
10. *Taki* – Japanese
11. *Pogpo* – Korean
12. *Wodospad* – Polish
13. *Selale* – Turkish

Drink Me:
Niagara Falls Cocktail

This tasty cocktail, called Niagara Falls of course, couldn't be better served to help you erode your headaches after a long day.

Make It Right

1.5 oz vodka
1.5 oz orange liqueur
Good dash of lemon juice
2 tsp syrup
1.5 oz ginger ale

Serving Suggestion

Drown the vodka in the orange liqueur, lemon juice and syrup in a shaker with ice cubes.

Shake well – as if the shaker was a barrel falling down the Falls.

Strain the liquid into a chilled champagne flute. Splash in the ginger ale.

Niagara Falls can fill up an Olympic-size swimming pool in half a second.

Songs To Get Wet To: Waterfall Playlist

There's lots of classic songs about waterfalls. These are our top ten. Which one's your favourite?

1. "Waterfalls" – TLC

2. "Waterfalls" – Paul McCartney

3. "Every Teardrop is a Waterfall" – Coldplay

4. "Waterfall" – Stone Roses

5. "Waterfall" – 10cc

6. "Waterfall" – Electric Light Orchestra

7. "May This Be Love (aka Waterfall)" – Jimi Hendrix

8. "Waterfall" – Carly Simon

9. "Waterfall" – Peter Frampton

10. "Waterfall" – Bananarama

In 1895, Nikola Tesla beat rival Thomas Edison to switch on the world's first large-scale hydroelectric power plant at Niagara Falls, using his alternating current (AC). It was the first time electricity could be harnessed by water in vast quantities.

It changed the world forever. At the time, the *Niagara Falls Gazette* reported, "The turning of a switch in the big powerhouse at Niagara completed a circuit which caused the Niagara River to flow uphill."

"

One frequently only
finds out how really beautiful
a really beautiful woman is
after considerable acquaintance
with her and the rule applies
to Niagara Falls.

"

Mark Twain

December 1678

The year French explorer Louis Hennepin, a Belgian Roman Catholic priest, became one of the first Europeans to verify the majesty of the Falls.

Thankfully, he wrote down what he saw:

66

Betwixt the Lake Ontario and Erie,
there is a vast and prodigious Cadence
of Water which falls down after a
surprising and astonishing manner,
insomuch that the Universe does not
afford its parallel. The Waters which fall
from this horrible Precipice, do foam
and boyl after the most hideous manner
imaginable, making an outrageous
Noise, more terrible than that of
Thunder; for when the Wind blows out
of the South, their dismal roaring may
be heard more than Fifteen Leagues off.

99

66

When I first approached them it was with my face lifted toward the sky, for I thought I was going to see an Atlantic ocean pouring down thence over cloud-vexed Himalayan heights, a sea-green wall of water sixty miles front and six miles high, and so, when the toy reality came suddenly into view – that beruffled little wet apron hanging out to dry – the shock was too much for me, and I fell with a dull thud.

Yet slowly, surely, steadily, in the course of my fifteen visits, the proportions adjusted themselves to the facts, and I came at last to realize that a waterfall a hundred and sixty-five feet high and a quarter of a mile wide was an impressive thing.

99

Mark Twain

"

Right now the inside of my
head feels like Niagara Falls
without the noise, just this
mist and churning and no
real sense of where earth
ends and heaven begins.

"

Douglas Coupland

The word "Niagara" belonged
originally to the Iroquoian natives.
It isn't the only Native American
word that English "borrowed"…

Avocado
(from the Nahuatl word *ahuácatl*)

Barbecue
(from the Taino word *barbacoa*)

Persimmon
(from the Cree word *pasiminan*)

Piranha
(from the Tupi word *pirátsainha*)

Potato
(from the Taino word *batata*)

CHAPTER
TWO

Over the Edge

Niagara Falls is famous for many things – water, being the main one. But, look down from the top, and you'll see a litany of other awesome features waiting to be discovered behind the curtain of rushing waters. Just be careful not to get too close to the edge…

In a 2021 One Poll survey,
22 per cent – one in five! – of
Americans thought Niagara
Falls was in Iceland, not on the
New York/Canadian border.

Only 32 per cent
of those surveyed said the
correct answer.

32

The speed, in feet per second, of the water as it plunges over the edge of the river's edge atop Horseshoe Falls. The Niagara River rapids reach a maximum speed of around 68 mph.

Since 1951, any daredevil caught red-handed near the edge of the Falls will be arrested for "Stunting Without a License", a federal law in America and Canada. The current fine is $10,000.

A 2022 survey revealed
Niagara Falls as the fourth most
popular bucket-list destination
in the world for both the Baby
Boomer and Z Generations,
behind only the Great Barrier
Reef, Giza Pyramids and the
Northern Lights.

Over a third
of people aged 65+ declared
Niagara their No.1 dream
must-see destination.

14

The amount, in millions of years, of time it would take for all Earth's water to go over the falls.

12 million

The average amount of tourists Niagara Falls receives every year. Some recent years have seen more than 20 million.

Human beings are born with only two innate fears: the fear of falling (*basophobia*) and the fear of loud sounds (*ligyrophobia*). Niagara Falls contains both.

"

At last, fortissimo!

"

Douglas Coupland

The famous Austrian composer declared "Fortissimo!"
when he first clapped eyes on the Falls. In music, a
fortissimo is a passage which is marked to be played
very loudly!

66

From a drop of water,
a logician could infer
the possibility of an
Atlantic or a Niagara
without having seen
or heard of one or
the other.

99

Sherlock Holmes

“

Niagara Falls is simply a vast
unnecessary amount of water
going over the wrong way and
then falling over unnecessary
cliffs… The wonder would be
if the water did not fall!

”

Oscar Wilde

33 per cent

A 2018 study revealed that
only one in three U.S. residents
have been to Niagara Falls,
despite it being one of the
world's Top Five most visited
landmarks that year.

12

As of 2022, the amount of people who have survived an intentional, or accidental, fall over the Falls.

"

Niagara falls, Viagra rises.

"

Stewart Stafford

June 15, 2012

The date American acrobat, aerialist, daredevil and high wire artist Nikolas Wallenda became the first person to walk a tightrope *directly* across Niagara Falls.

It took Wallenda two years to gain the approval of both American and Canadian authorities to perform the stunt…with one condition: he wear a safety harness, the first in his career.

"My idea scenario would be a foggy day. I disappear into the mist, then appear on the other side. How cool would that be?" he said of his world-first.

"

Once a girl's seen
Superman in action,
Niagara Falls kind of
leaves you cold. You
know what I mean?

"

Superman II (1980)

66

Niagara Falls is the
hanging tongue on
the face of the earth,
drooling endlessly
over its own beauty.

99

Vinita Kinra

1882

The year that Niagara's vast
fast-flowing water first provided
hydroelectric power, four years
after the technology was
invented in England in 1878.

"

All trembling, I reached the Falls of Niagara, and oh, what a scene! My blood shudders still, although I am not a coward, at the grandeur of the Creator's power and I gazed motionless on this new display of the irresistible force of one of his elements.

"

John James Audubon

"

When you're choosing somebody to handle a high-pressure job, you might want to go with the guy who won't get rattled. I was a stunt man. I was shot out of a cannon straight into Niagara Falls. Although, technically, I was supposed to go over Niagara 'Falls'?

"

Gonzo, *The Muppets*, "Pig's in a Blackout" (2015)

In terms of volume of water carried per mile, Niagara River is the largest river on the planet. For 22 miles, the river transports the entire content of North America's four Great Lakes – Lake Superior, Lake Michigan, Lake Huron and Lake Erie – before plunging over the Falls. One-fifth of all the fresh water on Earth is found in these four lakes.

Lake Superior, Lake Michigan
Lake Huron and Lake Erie, the
four North American lakes,
empty into Lake Ontario.
If spread out, the volume of
water in the Great Lakes would
cover North America in about
one metre (3.5 feet) of water!

Niagara

A French rock band, formed in 1982, that became stars in both France and Canada in the 1980s and early 1990s.

They had a hit single in 1985 called "Tchiki Boum". Somewhat bizarrely, the band took their name not from the Falls themselves, but the 1953 film of the same name starring Marilyn Monroe.

June 30, 1859

On this date, foolhardy Frenchman and funambulist Charles Blondin walked into history as the first man to tightrope across Niagara Falls, blowing the doors of human imagination and ingenuity wide open. It took him 23 minutes.

Blondin died at the age of 72, from diabetes.

Ten men and one woman
(Maria Spelterini) have walked a tightrope
across Niagara Falls since 1859:

1. Charles Blondin, 1859
2. Henry Bellini, 1873
3. Clifford Calverley, 1887
4. Samuel J. Dixon, 1891
5. William Hunt, 1860
6. Andrew Jenkins, 1869
7. Stephen Peer, 1887
8. Henri J. Rechatin, 1975
9. Maria Spelterini, 1876
10. James Hardy, 1896
11. Nik Wallenda, 2012

Niagara

A 1953 American thriller, directed by Henry Hathaway, starring Marilyn Monroe, Joseph Cotten, Jean Peters and Max Showalter. It was one of the year's biggest box-office hits. The movie's poster called the film, "Marilyn Monroe and Niagara – a raging torrent of emotion that even nature can't control!" and "the high-water mark in suspense!"

Pun intended, presumably.

Funambulus

The Latin word for "tightrope walker" is sadly not derived from "fun" and "amble", or funny walk. It comes from the Latin funis, meaning "rope", and *ambulare*, "to walk".

Horseshoe Falls

Named after its iconic U-bend, Horseshoe Falls is the mightiest of the three falls.

2,200 feet (670 metres) wide

167 feet (50 metres) tall

685,000 gallons of water per second

Today, approximately 50,000 newly-wed couples visit Niagara Falls each year. Many choose to sign their names in register books that are kept by the Niagara Falls Tourism Office, which have been digitized and indexed for this collection.

Niagara Falls was formed more than 12,000 years ago, following the end of the last Ice Age. Back then, Canada's land mass was densely squashed and carved by glaciers. As ice melted, new landscapes, lakes and rivers and waterfalls were created in its absence. Only 1 per cent of Canada's Great Lakes is rainwater; the rest is "fossil water" dating back to the Ice Age.

On January 11, 1909, America
and Canada finally entered
into an agreement to prevent
and resolve the lengthy
transboundary disputes over the
use of the waters shared by both
nations. The Boundary Waters
Treaty was signed to ensure
the use of Niagara River, and
its demand for hydroelectric
power, was shared appropriately,
while "safeguarding the unique
natural beauty of Niagara Falls".

It was Samuel de Champlain who, in 1604, became the first person to scribble a note about Niagara Falls. He wrote: "That there was a fall about a league wide and a large mass of water falls into said lake: that when this fall is passed one sees no more land on either side but only a sea so large that they have never seen the end of it, nor heard that anyone has…"

Honymoone

If you go to Niagara on your
honeymoon, don't forget to pack
your fermented honey booze!
The word "Honeymoon" is
derived from the Scandinavian
practice of imbibing this
alcoholic sweet milk during the
first month – or moon cycle
– of marriage to improve the
chances of conception.

In the 1950s, Niagara Falls was nicknamed "Baby City" after a record number of honeymooners conceived their first child at the World's Honeymoon Capital.

Niagara Falls is home to twin cities with the same name – Niagara Falls, Ontario, and, across the river, Niagara Falls, New York. But there are seven other cities in America with the name "Niagara" too.

1. Niagara, Wisconsin

2. Niagara, Virginia

3. Niagara, Pennsylvania

4. Niagara, Oregon

5. Niagara, North Dakota

6. Niagara, North Carolina

7. Niagara, Kentucky

In Season 6 of *The Office* – the world's most beloved comedy TV show – couple Pam and Jim said "I do" on a *Maid of the Mist* boat tour, in an episode entitled "Niagara".

66

Niagara Falls used to
be, like, a spiritual
experience for people.
They stayed in tents
and it blew their minds.
It's really kitschy now,
which is a lot of fun.

99

Jim Halpert, *The Office*, "Niagara"

CHAPTER
THREE

Barrel of Laughs

There are, perhaps, only two places on earth synonymous with barrels – wineries and Niagara Falls. For decades, this sacred spot became a haven for those wishing to see the Falls from a different perspective – the bottom! Time to get wet and see what all the fuss is about…

> 66
>
> This is what you call a sight of wonder. It's the only waterfall I know the name of.
>
> 99

J-Hope, member of the world's bestselling pop band, BTS

66

By what mysterious power is it that millions and millions are drawn from all parts of the world to gaze upon Niagara Falls! There is no mystery about the thing itself. Every effect is just such as any intelligent man, knowing the causes would anticipate, without seeing it.

99

Abraham Lincoln

The original "Maid of the Mist" was Lelawala, a beautiful maiden of the Native American Ongiara tribe. According to the tribe's legend, one day Lelawala fell out of her canoe as she was floating down the Niagara River. Heno, the Thunder God, who resides behind the Falls (and who's voice creates the water's deafening roar), rescued Lelawala.

Then, a giant venomous snake
went to attack Lelawala, but
Heno threw a lightning bolt at
the snake. Defeated, the snake
landed on top of the water, its
impact reshaping the river and
giving it the horseshoe shape
we know and love – and stay
well-clear of – today.

The now-iconic *Maid of the Mist* sightseeing boat had its maiden voyage on May 27, 1846.

Today, the two catamaran-style vessels are powered by electric and can carry more than 300 passengers per tour.

That's more than 1.85 million passengers a year.

There are three colours of recyclable ponchos on offer at the Falls, depending on which attraction you choose.

Maid of the Mist – **BLUE**

Hornblower Cruises – **RED**

Journey Behind the Falls – **YELLOW**

Niagara's Fury 4D – **BLUE**

"

As breath-taking as our
geography can be – you can't
visit the Niagara Falls and not
be impressed by the sights and
the sounds – it's our people
who make Canada great and
worth visiting.

"

Justin Trudeau

The Niagara River plunges over a cliff made of dolostone, limestone, shale and sandstone. These rocks were deposited here around 440 million years ago, when a shallow sea covered most of the eastern U.S. and Canada. Dolostone is made from the calcium-carbonate shells of dead aquatic micro-organisms called foraminifera, piling up to form sediment.

Bobby Leach, the second man who survived his barrel roll over Niagara Falls, died from complications sustained after slipping on an orange peel.

Barrel Daredevils of Niagara Falls

1. Annie Edson Taylor, 1901
2. Bobby Leach, 1911
3. Charles Stephens, 1920 – died
4. Jean Lussier, 1928
5. George Stathakis, 1930 – died
6. William Hill, 1951 – died
7. Nathan Boya, 1961
8. Karel Soucek, 1984
9. Steve Trotter, 1985
10. John Munday, 1985
11. Peter De Bernardi and Jeffery James Petkovich, 1989
12. Steve Trotter and Lori Martin, 1995

One-quarter

Hydroelectric power stations
along the Niagara River supply
more than one-quarter of all
power used in Ontario and
New York State, including
Manhattan's Times Square,
which requires 161 megawatts of
electricity every year!

Peter De Bernardi and Jeffery Petkovich were the first duo to go over the Horseshoe Falls. They used a 12-foot, 3000 lb steel barrel. The stunt was performed to raise awareness for an anti-drugs campaign. The barrel was inscribed with the words, "Don't put yourself on the Edge – Drugs will kill you!"

"

The prettiest Sunday afternoon drive in the world.

"

Sir Winston Churchill, about the Niagara Parkway, a scenic route that stretches for 56 km (35 miles) from Fort Erie, past the Falls to Fort George.

Niagara Falls is home to many world-class casinos, attractions that draw more than 6 million people a year. In 2004, a Toronto tax accountant, Nick Hulst, won $5.8 million at Niagara Fallsview Casino Resort, the largest jackpot in Canadian history! Hulst spent $60 on a Megabucks slot machine and, on the 20th spin, walked away a multi-millionaire.

66

It is not for me to attempt
a description of Niagara; I
feel I have no powers for it.
There is a shadowy mystery
that hangs about it which
neither the eye nor even the
imagination can penetrate.

99

Frances Trollope

66

When this prodigious quantity of water, of which I speak, comes to fall, there is such a din, and such a noise, that it is more deafening than the loudest thunder.

99

Louis Hennepin

1801

The first year a newly-wed couple went on a "bridal tour" to Niagara Falls. The bride was 18-year-old Theodosia Burr, the daughter of U.S. Vice President Aaron Burr, and wealthy landowner, Joseph Alston. News spread of the famous couple's jaunt, and soon enough it became the thing for married couples to do. Apart from make love, of course.

French Emperor Napoleon Bonaparte's younger brother, Jerome Bonaparte, honeymooned at Niagara Falls with his American bride, Elizabeth Patterson, in 1804. They made the 1,200-mile bumpy ride to the Falls from New Orleans by stagecoach, a journey that was so perilous it has become the stuff of legend, further boosting Niagara's worldwide lure.

"

Are you the fool that's going over the Falls?

"

Mighellis Butler, Mayor of Niagara Falls, 1893-94,
to Annie Edison Taylor

Funambulist and Niagara-
native Stephen Peer tumbled
45 feet to his death in 1887,
three days after he first
successfully walked on a wire
cable stretched across the gorge.
He had been drinking with his
friends when he attempted
this feat.

Talk about Peer pressure!

For 30 years, Charles Blondin fun-ambled across Niagara more than 300 times.

Tightrope-walking more than 10,000 miles (16,000 km), in his lifetime, the equivelent of walking from the UK to Australia!

With each trip he increased
his trickery: he took photos,
he laid down, performed
flips and somersaults, walked
backwards, wore a sack on his
head, fired a gun, was shot at,
wore a monkey suit, traipsed
with a wheelbarrow, carried
his manager on his back,
was shackled, on stilts, ate
cake, drank champagne and,
finally, cooked an omelette
on an iron stove.

Mark Twain called
Charles Blondin an
"adventurous ass".

Niagara Falls tourism adds $2.4 billion annually to the local economy.

82 per cent

In 2021, a survey asked adults in the U.S. about how they viewed popular tourist attractions. Niagara Falls ranked first, with a positivity score of 82 per cent. (Yellowstone National Park and Grand Canyon National Park came joint second with 81 per cent.)

Niagara Falls is more than just a beautiful waterfall.

There are also more than 2,800 Falls-themed places to go, including 1,231 full-service restaurants, 178 hotels and motels, 153 bed and breakfasts, 109 arts venues, 97 wineries and 43 golf courses.

Today, 65 per cent of all Niagara Falls tourists come from within Canada. 25 per cent are from the United States, and 10 per cent come from overseas.

66

Let me tell you something. You're young, you're in love. Well, I'll give you a warning. Don't let it get out of hand, like those Falls out there. Up above. Did you ever see the river up above the Falls? It's calm, and easy, and you throw in a log, it just floats around. Let it move a little further down and it gets going faster, hits some rocks, and… in a minute it's in the lower rapids, and… nothing in the world – including God himself, I suppose – can keep it from going over the edge. It just – *goes*.

99

George Loomis, *Niagara*, 1953

CHAPTER
FOUR

Angels and Daredevils

For the better part of a century, death-defying daredevils, funambulists and thrill-seekers were called – lured? – to Niagara to perform thousands of outrageous, and dangerous, stunts – many of which have become as famous as the Falls themselves, much to Mother Nature's envy.

October 1, 1995

On this fateful day, stuntman Robert Overacker became the first daredevil to ride a jet ski over the edge of Horseshoe Falls.

His parachute failed to open and Robert plummeted into the rocks below. His body was never recovered.

Following the death of barrel-roller William "Red" Hill, Jr. in 1951, anyone caught in the act of "stunting without a license" will be arrested and subject to fines of up to $25,000 USD in accordance with the Niagara Parks Act.

In 1990, world-famous illusionist David Copperfield performed his "Niagara Falls Challenge".

For this feat, Copperfield is tied in chains inside a yellow box, suspended in mid-air above a wooden raft. The raft is then set on fire and airlifted to the middle of the Niagara River 152 meters (500 feet) from the edge of the Falls.

For the trick to work, Copperfield had one minute to escape the box and jet ski to safety. However, the flaming raft goes over the edge of the Falls with Copperfield supposedly still inside. Moments later, Copperfield can be seen dangling from a wire connected to a helicopter, alive and well.

Even more magically, Copperfield's black leather jacket doesn't even appear to get wet at all.

Niagara Falls is not technically owned by either of the two countries it straddles. There is only an agreed geographical boundary.

The Horseshoe Falls is Canadian, and the American and Bridal Falls are American.

In 2012, when daredevil Nik Wallenda tightrope-walked from one side of the Falls to the other, he carried his passport with him and had to present it upon reaching the Canadian side.

9,046,145

The amount, in 355ml cans of Coca-Cola, that plunge over the falls every second.

That's 542,768,700 every minute!

16,056,908

The number of times you'd have to go for a wee to equal the amount of water that falls over Niagara *every second*.

(Obviously, not every wee is the same volume, so we've used a 200ml average.)

Every minute = 963,414,480!!

Every hour = 57,804,868,800!!!

The word "Niagara" derives from the Native American Iroquoian word "Onguiaahra", meaning "Neck of the Land".

The reason the Iroquoians called the Falls a "neck" is because the Niagara River, unlike all other rivers in this part of Canada, flows north (not south, like most rivers), connecting two large bodies of water together – Lake Erie and Lake Ontario.

nai·a·gruh

The proper way to pronounce
Niagara. (Not nia-grah – note the
stress on the second "a".)

The name "Niagara" first appears as "Onguiaahra" on the maps recorded by Jesuit priest, Jérôme Lalemant, in 1641.

The first time the standardized spelling of "Niagara" was first used was on Hermann Moll's "The Great Fall of Niagara" map of 1715.

Bridal Veil Falls

Situated on the American side, Bridal Veil Falls derives its name from the strong winds which blow the waterfall into a sideways mist that looks like a bride's veil. Native Americans called it Pohono – "Spirit of the Puffing Wind".

56 feet (17 metres) wide

78 feet (24 metres) tall

75,000 gallons of water per second

50 per cent

Chances of a wish coming true if you throw a coin into the Falls.*

* In June 1969, Niagara was drained for the first time ever. Millions of coins were found and had to be carried out in hundreds of large buckets.

Katarraktiphobia

The fear of waterfalls.

20-30

The average amount of people who choose to commit suicide every year by jumping over the edge of the Falls.

For centuries, it has been said that Niagara's falling water is so hypnotic that visitors can get the uncontrollable urge to hurl themselves into the watery void. This phenomenon, coined first by the French, is named *L'appel du Vide*, or... the Call of the Void.

Indeed, the first non-Native to bear witness to the Falls, awesomeness, Louis Hennepin, wrote of this trance-like allure. "The temptation to throw one's self down this incredible precipice is almost too great for resistance," he wrote in 1678.

Franglais

The only nine-letter anagram of Niagara Falls.

(And, no doubt, the form of English spoken by tourists on the Canadian side.)

66

I went to Niagara Falls
with my family when
I was young, and I cried
because I thought it
would be bigger.

99

Meryl Davis

66

No horse gets anywhere until
he is harnessed. No stream or gas
drives anything until it is
confined. No Niagara is ever
turned into light and power until
it is tunnelled. No life ever
grows great until it is focused,
dedicated, disciplined.

99

Harry Emerson Fosdick

"

I was disappointed in
Niagara – most people must
be disappointed in Niagara.
Every American bride is taken
there and the sight of the
stupendous waterfall must be
one of the earliest, if not the
keenest, disappointments in
American married life.

"

Oscar Wilde

The "Niagara of the East", Fukiware Falls is located in Japan's Gunma prefecture.

This outstanding natural beauty is a 7-meter-high, 30-metre-wide waterfall, surrounded by odd-shaped boulders set against the luscious forests of Katashina Ravine.

Thalassophobia

The persistent and intense fear
of deep bodies of water.

On July 4, 1930, George Stathakis and his 105-year-old pet turtle, Sonny Boy, took a leap of faith over the Horseshoe Falls in a barrel. They both survived the fall.

However, Stathakis's barrel got stuck behind the Falls for fourteen hours and he ran out of oxygen and perished. Sonny Boy lived.

66

Everybody goes to Niagara Falls.

99

Just This Once (1952)

Aquaphobia

The fear of water.

"

Something borrowed,
something blue – old, new!
Rice and old shoes, carry you
over the threshold, Niagara
Falls – all the silly tripe I've
made fun of for years.

"

Arsenic and Old Lace (1944)

> **"**
>
> Niagara Falls is very nice. I'm very glad I saw it, because from now on if I am asked whether I have seen Niagara Falls I can say yes and be telling the truth for once.
>
> **"**

John Steinbeck

"

It would be hard for a man to stand nearer God than he does there. There was a bright rainbow at my feet; and from that I looked up to – great Heaven! to what a fall of bright green water! The broad, deep, mighty stream seems to die in the act of falling; and, from its unfathomable grave, arises that tremendous ghost of spray and mist which is never laid, and has been haunting this place with the same dread solemnity – perhaps from the creation of the world. Whenever I think of Niagara, I shall think of its beauty.

"

Charles Dickens

In 1901, Annie Edson Taylor, a blind and seriously unwell 63-year-old school teacher, became the first person to go over the Niagara Falls in a barrel. She hoped her stunt would make her famous. She was found alive 17 minutes after her plunge.

"If it was with my dying breath, I would caution anyone against attempting the feat," Taylor said afterwards. "I would sooner walk up to the mouth of a cannon knowing it was going to blow me to pieces than make another trip over the Falls."

Taylor died penniless in 1921.

She was buried in Niagara Falls' Oakwood Cemetery in a plot called Stunters' Rest, later to be kept company by fellow Niagara Falls daredevils.

Her tombstone reads, "Annie Edson Taylor: First to go over Horseshoe Falls in a barrel and live, Oct. 4, 1901."

Iagara, the cat

Annie Edison Taylor's pet cat was the first animal (presumably) to survive falling over the Falls in a barrel.

Annie tested the barrel-and-cat combo before her infamous plummet a few days later.

Thankfully, Iagara was unscathed by the trip. Physically, at least.

Petraphobia

The fear of rocks

1,714

The number of lightning strikes required to generate 2.4 million kilowatts of electricity – the same as the Niagara Falls hydroelectric power plant.

1,408

The number of days it would take to fill up the Grand Canyon with the two quadrillion gallons required from Niagara Falls' flow rate.

25 per cent

The chances of surviving a daredevil attempt over, or across, the Falls.

Scientists have speculated that the American Falls could run dry within the next 2,000 years due to a process known as Isostatic rebound, which could cause the Falls to lift up as ice melts.

More than 100 Hollywood movies and TV shows, and scores of documentaries, have employed Niagara Falls as the background to their stories.

These are the Top 10 best known.

1. *Bruce Almighty (2004)*

2. *Pirates of the Caribbean: At World's End (2007)*

3. *What Dreams May Come (1998)*

4. *Dead Man (1995)*

5. *Hudson Hawk (1991)*

6. *Canadian Bacon (1995)*

7. *Luv (1967)*

8. *Niagara (1953)*

9. *Superman II (1980)*

10. *The Dead Zone (1983)*

American Falls

With Bridal Veil Falls, the American Falls offers just 10 per cent of Niagara's waterflow, and it sits slightly elevated above the Horseshoe Falls.

830 feet (250 meters) wide

176 feet (53.6 meters) tall

150,000 gallons of water per second

CHAPTER
FIVE

Rise and Fall

Once upon a time, Niagara Falls
was a beacon that lit up the world, a
Honeymoon Capital and domain of the
daredevil. Today, this icon of wonder is
the grandmaster of tourism, offering a
host of things to see and do beyond the
Falls and breathing new life into this
400 million-year-old freak of nature.

Enochlophobia

The fear of large groups
of people.

“

Two tickets to
Niagara Falls, eh? How
romantic. That's where
honeymooners go.

”

Baby, Take a Bow (1934)

"

Niagara Falls is wet; so, take along your rubbers!

"

Bye Bye Birdie **(1963)**

“

It's easier sliding up
Niagara Falls than it is
to understand a woman.

„

The Plainsman (1936)

June 1969

As hippies across the U.S. turned on and dropped out, Niagara Falls was turned off.

For the three days, more than 1,200 U.S. Army Corps. of Engineers trucks dumped 28,000 tons of rocks upstream of the falls to divert the flow of the Niagara River away from American Falls. This "de-watering" was to study the effects of erosion. Two bodies and millions of coins were also found.

5,000

The number of dead bodies found at the foot of the Falls between 1850 and 2011.

Suicide was ruled as the main cause of the deaths.

1 foot

Niagara Falls is currently eroding at a rate of 1 foot every year. It could be reduced to 1 foot every 10 years if more water is diverted to generate more hydroelectric power, though that would greatly dimmish the Falls' thundering roar for visitors.

5.5. billion

The true power of Niagara's flow rate is 5.5 billion gallons of water of the Falls per hour. Today, visitors only ever see 25 to 50 per cent of the Falls' full capacity.

Often, up to 75 per cent of the Niagara River is diverted from going over the Falls to generate hydroelectric power. At night, the flow of the Falls' is reduced even more to allow more water to be used to generate hydroelectric power, and not interfere with tourists' prime visiting hours.

On March 29, 1848, all three of Niagara's falls were reduced to tiny "trickles" when ice jammed water flow upstream on the Niagara River.

90 per cent of the fish that go over the Falls survive. Fish can survive the leap of faith as their bodies can absorb a lot of pressure, unlike heavier humans. There's also a cushion of air bubbles at the bottom that softens the fall.

There are ninety-four species of fish in the Niagara River.

It was in her 1953 movie, *Niagara*, that Marilyn Monroe received her first star billing.

The film was also the first of three blockbusters the actress starred in in 1953 – alongside *Gentlemen Prefer Blondes* and *How to Marry a Millionaire* – the most successful year of her film career.

116 feet (of film)

In *Niagara*, Marilyn set a world record with her now-iconic walk away from camera (with Niagara in background, and her bottom firmly in the foreground), the longest walk in cinema history, lasting 26.92 seconds, and spooling 116 feet of film.

The third man to plunge over the Falls was John Lussier, on July 4, 1928.

No barrel this time. Instead, John went for a ride over the side in a six-foot rubber ball lined with inflated rubber tubes. Lussier survived and sold pieces of the ball's rubber tubes to earn some extra cash, one of the first kitschy souvenirs ever sold at Niagara.

But not the last.

"

I knew I was on the edge of the precipice, and braced myself for the shock, and I think that for about 3 seconds I lost my reason. I did not faint, but my mind was gone. I was oblivious of everything. The awful rolling knocks my head first on the front of the barrel and then on the back. I expected to be killed at any moment, but even at that I was not sorry that I was where I was.

"

Annie Edison Taylor

July 2, 1984

Karel Soucek, a Czech stuntman, was the last daredevil to go over the Falls in a barrel. His custom-made barrel bore the words, "Last of the Niagara Daredevils – 1984" and his motto: "It's not whether you fail or triumph, it's that you keep your word… and at least try!"

At a descent speed of 75 miles per hour (121 km/h), Soucek's barrel took 45 minutes to be recovered. The only injuries sustained were caused by his wristwatch hitting his face upon impact with the water.

Soucek died a few months later
performing a stunt

Evil Knievel called "the most
dangerous I've ever seen", when
Soucek was dropped inside a
barrel from 180 feet atop the
Houston Astrodome into a tank
of water.

In 1961, Nathan Boya became the first African American to ride the Falls in a barrel, and, awkwardly, the first to be fined for doing so under the Niagara Parks Act.

The reason Boya performed the stunt was not for fame or fortune. It was an act of penance for breaking off his engagement with his fiancée. Yes, Niagara Falls was their planned honeymoon destination.

66

You guys are like Butch and Sundance peering over the edge of a cliff to the boulder-filled rapids 300 feet below, thinking you better not jump 'cause there's a chance you might drown. The President has this disease and has been lying about it, and you guys are worried that the polling might make us look bad? It's the fall that's gonna kill ya.

99

CJ Cregg, *The West Wing*, 'The Fall's Gonna Kill You'

July 9, 1960

Roger Woodward, a seven-year-old, accidently fell over Horseshoe Falls after falling out of his boat further upstream on the Niagara River. He was wearing a life jacket. The boy became the first person to survive the fall without protection from a barrel.

"I was floating in a cloud," the boy told the world's media years later. "I had no sensation of up or down. I didn't have any sensation in my stomach like you might have on a roller coaster… that moment when your stomach is in your throat."

October 2003

Kirk Jones became the first recorded adult to survive a jump over Horseshoe Falls. As hundreds of tourists screamed in horror, Jones plunged feet first. He described the feeling of being in the waters below the Falls: "It felt like a team of people were beating me with baseball bats." He suffered two fractured ribs and bruised vertebrae. He was later arrested and banned for life from the Falls.

Jones repeated the attempt in 2017 in an inflatable ball with his pet boa constrictor, Misty. He died.

In July 2019, at 4am, a man was seen by Niagara Park police vanishing over Horseshoe Falls in an apparent attempt to end his life.

He was found alive a few hours later sitting on rocks near the edge of the river. "He's a very lucky guy. Not many people do it and survive," reported the *Buffalo News*. "He definitely had God in his top pocket."

"

There are others so constituted
as to be fascinated by the
spectacle to such a dangerous
and overpowering extent, as
to feel a strong desire to throw
themselves into the abyss.

"

Walter Henry

CHAPTER
SIX

Leap of Faith

Welcome to the end of the tour!
Remember to recycle your poncho.
But before we go home, let's take one
last leap of faith into the unknown
down ol' Niagara. Who knows, you
may fall in love all over again…

"

It seems that I have always
been ahead of my time. I had
to wait nineteen years before
Niagara was harnessed by my
system, fifteen years before the
basic inventions for wireless
which I gave to the world in
1893 were applied universally.

"

Nikola Tesla

"

Getting information
from the internet is like
getting a glass of water
from the Niagara Falls.

"

Arthur C. Clarke

"

Their roar is around me. I am on the brink Of the great waters— and their anthem voice Goes up amid the rainbow and the mist.

"

Grenville Mellen, "Niagara", 1893.

"

You can descend a staircase here
a hundred and fifty feet down
and stand at the edge of the
water. After you have done it,
you will wonder why you did it;
but you will then be too late.

"

Mark Twain

"

I've been in the barrel tumbling down Niagara Falls… and I emerged, and I lived, and that's such a liberating feeling.

"

Barack Obama (on being President for eight years).

66

I could more easily contain Niagara Falls in a teacup than I can comprehend the wild, uncontainable love of God.

99

Brennan Manning

"

I was whirled around at lightning speed, and then I crashed into the rocks three times — oh, my head, my head! Nobody ought to do that again.

"

Annie Edson Taylor

"

As a youth, I was fascinated by a
description of Niagara Falls
I had perused and pictured in my
imagination a big wheel run by the
Falls. I told my uncle that I would
go to America and carry out this
scheme. Thirty years later I saw
my ideas carried out at Niagara
and marvelled at the unfathomable
mystery of the mind.

"

Nikola Tesla

Today, Niagara Falls constantly produces more than 2.4 million kilowatts of electricity, enough to power 24 million 100-watt lightbulbs at once.

"

There are three things I'll never forget about America: the Rocky Mountains, Niagara Falls and Amos and Andy.

"

George Bernard Shaw

"

When we leave here and go up to
Niagara Falls, we are representing
Dunder Mifflin, everyone. This is
a very important wedding for the
branch. The most important wedding
until I get married. So, I want you
all on your best behaviour or so
help me, God. So… I will see you
up there in Viagra Falls!

"

Michael Scott, *The Office*, "Niagara"

While Niagara Falls is almost precisely the same height as Nelson's Column in London's Trafalgar Square, the river beneath its feet plunges another 56.6 metres (185 feet) on average.

Were you to jump off the top of Niagara Falls, you would almost certainly hit the bottom of the river.

Niagara Falls is part of the Niagara Falls State Park, which is the oldest state park in America, established in 1885 as the Niagara Reservation.

The park was designed by Frederick Law Olmsted, who also designed New York City's Central Park.

Today, there are more than 10,000 state park areas across the U.S.'s 50 states.

Argentina's Iguazu Falls is twice as tall as Niagara Falls' 50 metres.

The world's largest waterfalls is Venezuela's Angel Falls, with a plunge of more than 800 metres!

Like Niagara itself, waterfalls are divided into two categories: **Cataract** and **Cascade**.

Niagara Falls is classified as a Cataract due to its "large, single vertical drop falling clear of the bedrock".

A Cascade waterfall describes "water running over an irregular steep surfaced gradient where the water is generally in contact with the river bedrock".

For two centuries,
Niagara Falls was considered
the "Honeymoon Capital of
the World".

Today, 50,000 couples
get married at Niagara Falls
each year.

"

She watched the circling swirl of the eddies, and whirlpools and the mighty downpour of the falls till her weak nerves were wrought with an unconquerable desire to rush along with the waves. She fancied they had a message for her.

"

Dr A. L. Benedict, about a patient of his who committed suicide at Niagara.

66

Oh, the lovers come a
thousand miles,

They leave their home
and mother;

Yet when they reach
Niagara Falls

They only see each other.

99

"Niagara Falls", Anonymous, 1841

In 2019, *At the Brink*, a suicide documentary by Niagara journalist Michael Clarkson, claimed that while during her thriller *Niagara* in 1952, Marilyn Monroe was seen twice stepping onto the railing near Horseshoe Falls, seemingly lured by the water.

A decade later, in 1962, Monroe died from an overdose of sleeping pills (barbiturates) in L.A. Her death was ruled a probable suicide.

Superman II's Lois Lane,
actress Margot Kidder
reportedly told an extra while
filming the 1980 superhero
film, "I can see why people
jump. There's a draw to the
water. I feel like it's pulling me."

Kidder's death was ruled a
suicide in 2018.

> **"**
>
> They look at the water, and the next thing you know they're wading out and over they go.
>
> **"**

Captain Bruce Wright, Niagara County Sheriff's Marine Unit

66

The sound is of thunder in its greatest intensity ... It would be heard amid the roaring of a volcano, and yet does not drown the chirping of a sparrow.

99

Thomas Hamilton

On September 27, 1993, daredevil David Munday became the first person to go over the Falls twice, following his successful attempt in 1985.

It later turned out that David couldn't swim.

66

I do not wish to be classed with women who are seeking notoriety. I am not going over the Falls as a mere act of bravado. I feel that something may accrue from it in a financial way.

99

Annie Edison Taylor

"

As the barrel approached the brink, the multitude of voices hushed, as if by magic, and the silence was intense as the fearful plunge was made. Not a sound was heard except for the roar of the cataract until 'there he is' was shouted by dozens of voices as the barrel reappeared in the seething, bubbling waters below, some little distance below the falls.

"

Niagara Falls Ontario. Daily Record reporter described the moment Bobby Leach plunged over the Falls.

Daredevil Charles Stephens, from Bristol, England, was the first European to go over the side in a barrel. Stephens ignored pleas from fellow stuntmen to test his barrel beforehand.

He paid the price. The barrel broke apart and the only part of Stephens to be recovered from the wreckage was his right arm. Daredevilin' – not exactly a barrel of laughs, is it?

"

It's Niagara Falls.
It's one of the most
beautiful natural
wonders in the world.
Who wouldn't want
to walk across it?

"

Nikolas Wallenda